# The Story of a Sweet Gum

*The Story of a Sweet Gum*
by Sarah Hubbard
art by Sarah Cook

*The Story of a Sweet Gum*
Copyright © 2016
by Sarah Hubbard
Art by Sarah Cook

All rights reserved. All characters featured in this work of fiction and
the distinctive names and likenesses thereof, and all related indicia are properties of Sarah Hubbard.
No similarity between the names, characters, persons, or institutions, and any such actual entities is intended,
and any such similarity which may exist is purely coincidental.

No portion of this book may be reproduced by any means without the express written consent
of the copyright holders, except brief passages
used in connection with a review.

For advertising, licensing, orders, or other inquiries, please visit
www.garbagefactory.com

Packaged and Published by
The Garbage Factory
Athens, Georgia, USA

If you are unable to order this book from your local bookseller, you may order directly from the publisher.
Visit www.garbagefactory.com or www.listeningtosilence.com for contact information.

ISBN 978-0-9975227-3-0

10 9 8 7 6 5 4 3 2 1

*To Earth,
Our Greatest Teacher*

*I sat and watched a leaf grow on a Sweet Gum Tree.*

*It began growing when this tree was just a seed itself.
Dropped by its parent from somewhere in the canopy of leaves.*

*It could have landed anywhere
Yet this is where it settled.*

*As the time passed and the seed lay upon the earth,
The light became dark.
The trees around it dropped their leaves,
Covering the ground upon which the seed lay
In blankets of browns, golds, reds, and oranges.*

*The nights became longer.*
*The air became cold.*
*The seed was well protected,*
*Having all that it would need to survive the first winter*
*Stored within its soft shell.*

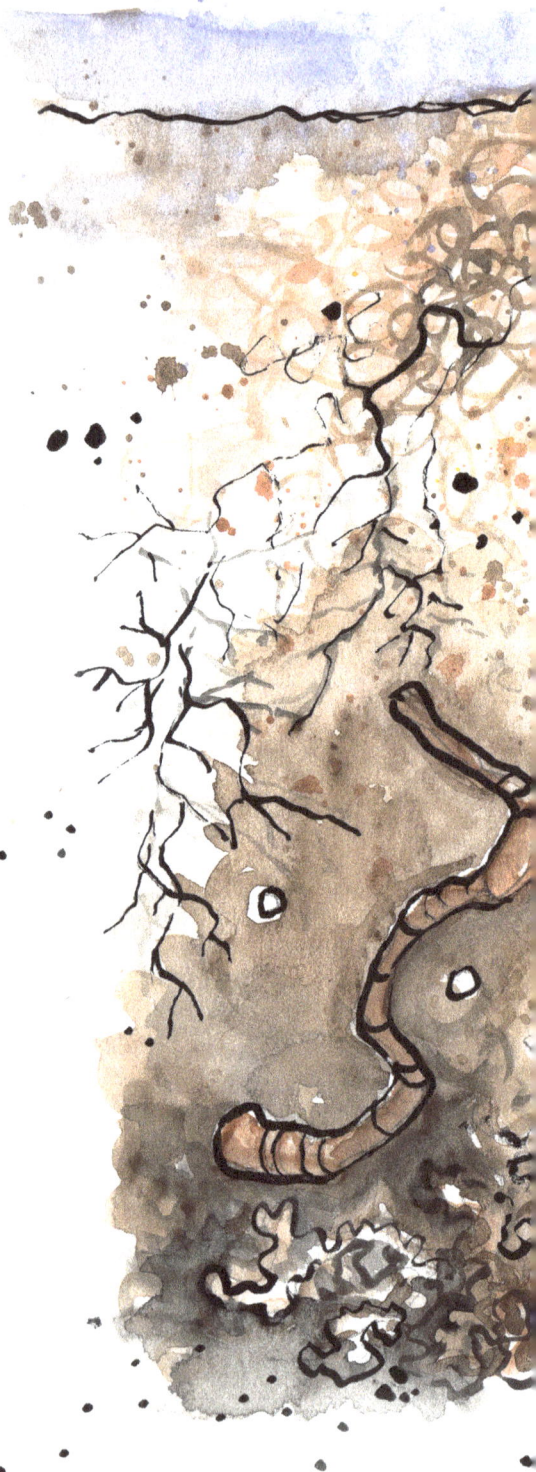

*In the latest part of the winter,
The light began to grow longer.
Brighter.
Warmer.
Sweet soft bird song filled the
   morning breeze.*

Earth began to stir,
Calling the seed into action.
It rumbled within the shell
And burst forth through the layers of leaves,
A tender young shoot of a Sweet Gum Tree.

Its life in that moment became more than a possibility.

*During the very first growing season,*
*Every atom of its fragile body worked towards growth.*

*In its first Spring,*
*It labored towards the light*
*And with its tender young roots it reached deeper into the earth.*

*Earth made its way through its
   orbit, closer to the sun
Causing the days to grow longer
And warmer.
The delicate Sweet Gum Shoot
Absorbed all the sunlight its first
   leaves could.*

*It wasn't easy to find the light
Under the giant leaves of the oaks,
the poplars,
and the dogwoods.*

*As Earth reached the climax of
  her orbit,
Arriving as close to the sun as
  she would,
Summer came to this spot in
  the woods,
Bringing with it sweltering heat
And powerful thunderstorms.
The Sweet Gum Sapling did all
  that it could do.
It grew.*

*As the sun bared down upon
   the Earth,
The water held within the
   leaves of the Sweet Gum Tree
Evaporated quickly.
The leaves began to dry out.
Their bright green color
   changed
To vibrant shades of reds and
   browns.*

With the arrival of fall,
The sun's light had a subtle change.
It became softer.
Its leaves fell to the forest floor,
Blanketing seeds that, like itself, had landed upon the surface of earth.

While Earth spun towards winter,
The Sweet Gum Sapling's tender outer layer
Began to harden into the bark that would protect it
For all the coming years of growth.

*While winter reigned the Earth,
The Sweet Gum stood in what
   seemed like stillness
And yet it grew.*

*Seasons came and went.
Years passed.
The Sweet Gum grew taller.
It grew stronger.
Until one winter day ...*

*... As the sun rose
A little green bud first appeared
   on a branch of the young tree.*

*As Earth moved in her orbit toward the sun
The bud swelled and filled with color.*

*With the help of the birds calling it forward in the early spring,
Each day the little green bud grew larger,
Until, just like the seed, it burst forth,
Unraveling into the leaf that I sat here and watched grow.*

*Insects zoom around the leaf.
It dances in the breeze.
Sunlight reflects off its thin surface.*

*Water droplets sparkle with precarious balance.
Birds come to the branch from which it hangs.*

*It is more than just a leaf on a Sweet Gum Tree*

*It is alive....*

*... It is the Universe
Perfectly packaged into this moment.*

# About the Author and the Artist

**Sarah Hubbard** likes to wear dangly earrings and lie on the ground while clouds drift easily across the sky. She creates if she is awake. She writes, she takes pictures, she daydreams.... She talks to spiders, birds, and worms. She loves children and hangs out with them whenever she can. She meditates and read obsessively to learn the way of stillness--of silence.

She lives in Athens, GA, where her roots run deep like a wolf tree. A true Southerner, she enjoys iced sweet tea under the pines with her two children and he beloved husband DirtPunk. She is a self-diagnosed pathological Earth-lover, and like her teachers, the trees, she is always reaching towards the light while standing firmly planted in the soil that surrounds her.

**Sarah Cook** writes:

My journey as an artist began when I was a little girl. I found such rapture in drawing and could lose myself in that other world that was mine alone. However, constantly creating images of what I saw in that world also allowed others to be a part of it. Time seems to stand still when I am drawing or painting.

I consider myself a folk artist. Although I have had no real formal training, I have been a student of life and observing everyone and everything as my master and teacher. I am very appreciative for the opportunities that have presented themselves to me so seamlessly, for what I have learned from them, and for the enthusiastic approval with which my creations are received.

www.ingramcontent.com/pod-product-compliance
Lightning Source LLC
Chambersburg PA
CBHW061936290426
44113CB00025B/2936